Seymour Simon's Book of
TRUCKS

HARPERCOLLINSPUBLISHERS

Trucks do all kinds of jobs. They do farm work. They help build buildings and roads. They help fight fires. They deliver mail. They transport food, clothing, furniture, toys, and books. Trucks are specially designed to carry heavy loads. The front of this truck is protected by a steel bumper and grille.

Trucks come in all shapes and sizes. Some trucks are bigger than the biggest dinosaur that ever lived. Trucks can weigh as much as ten elephants put together. This giant truck carries a house to a new building site.

Log Truck

A log truck carries cut-up tree trunks. The logs are held in place by metal poles and cables. The truck brings the logs to a sawmill. A crane picks up the logs with its steel jaws and stacks them in huge piles. At the sawmill, the bark is stripped from the logs, and the logs are cut into wooden boards called lumber.

Cement Mixer

A cement mixer carries the cement used to make roads and buildings. The mixing drum contains concrete—a mixture of cement, sand, and water. As the truck is driven to the construction site, its drum slowly turns to prevent the wet cargo from setting. The drum turns in one direction when the concrete is being mixed. The drum tilts up and turns in the other direction when it pours out the concrete.

Telescoping Forklift Truck

A telescoping forklift truck lifts building materials such as steel beams and bricks from the ground. The forklift has prongs like a fork. The operator slides the prongs under an object to be raised and moved. The telescoping arm adjusts to different heights. It can reach as high as the top of a small building. Some forklift trucks have gasoline engines. Smaller forklift trucks may be powered by electrical batteries.

Dump Truck

A dump truck carries heavy construction materials from one place to another. Power machines use large clamshell jaws to load a dump truck with rocks, earth, gravel, or sand. A dump truck this size can carry dirt that weighs more than one hundred people put together. When the truck reaches its destination, the driver raises the load carrier and dumps out the cargo exactly where it is needed.

Semitrailer Truck

A semitrailer truck is sometimes just called a semi. It has two parts: the tractor unit and the trailer. The tractor unit contains the engine and the cab. The engine is much more powerful than the engine of even the biggest car. The cab is where the driver sits.

Some cabs have a bed behind the front seat so that a driver on a long trip can pull off the road and get some sleep.

The trailer unit, which can have eight or more wheels, attaches to the tractor unit. It carries all kinds of cargo, from fruits and vegetables to TV sets and computers.

Flatbed Truck

This flatbed truck is carrying the space shuttle to a launch at the Cape Kennedy Space Center. Flatbed trucks can carry loads that would not fit into a box-shaped trailer, such as other trucks, tractors, boats, houses, and airplanes. On public roads, a flatbed truck carrying an oversize load travels slowly, escorted by cars traveling in front and behind. The escort cars carry signs that tell other drivers to be careful of the load on the truck.

Tractor

This tractor pulls a sprayer through rows of crops on a farm. It is a fast way to spray crops with fertilizers, which help plants grow, or insecticides, which get rid of the insects that may feed on the plants. Tractors pull many different farm machines, including plows, seeders, grass cutters, and hay bailers.

Buses

Buses are trucks that are specially designed to carry passengers. School buses take students back and forth between their homes and schools. They have safety-warning lights, stop signs, and flags that operate when the bus stops to pick up children. Some are also equipped with safety devices such as seat belts to make passengers as safe as possible.

Tanker Truck

This tanker truck carries liquid petroleum or oil. Other tanker trucks carry gasoline from refineries to gas stations and heating oil from oil storage tanks to homes. A refrigerated tanker truck carries milk from dairy farms to milk-processing and -bottling plants. Sometimes trucks on long-distance trips pull two tankers that are attached to each other.

Fire Engine Platform Truck

Fire trucks are designed to perform many different functions. This fire engine platform truck shoots water onto a burning building. Firefighters stand on the raised platform. The water hose is attached to a long arm, or boom, at the top of the platform. Another hose from the truck is attached to a nearby water hydrant. A pumping engine in the truck increases the pressure so that the water can reach far and high into the air. Firefighters climb the extending ladder on an aerial ladder truck to rescue people from burning buildings. Searchlight unit trucks are used to light a building at night.

Sanitation Truck

Sanitation trucks collect garbage and refuse. When fitted with rotating brushes, they can be used to clean streets. Some sanitation trucks, called sprinklers, contain water tanks that are large enough to wash down a road. Where it snows, sanitation

trucks are fitted with snowplows. They push snow aside and clear roads.

Road-Train Truck

This road-train truck pulls three or four trailers at the same time just the way a locomotive pulls freight cars on a train. Road-train trucks transport cargo in places where the distance between cities is enormous, such as in Australia. The trailers on a road train are attached to each other so that they can bend around a curve in a highway. Road trains are too big to enter the streets of a city. They load and unload their cargo at special stations outside cities.

Monster Truck

This powerful monster truck crushes cars at a truck show. Each monster truck is unique, because it is built by hand from other trucks and spare parts. Some monster trucks weigh as much as five elephants and have tires that are taller than a person. You can imagine what happens when a monster truck leaps across a row of cars and lands on the cars. SQUASH!

Trucks push and pull. They dig and dump. They sweep and shovel. They carry and crush. Every day. Everywhere.

To Joel, Benjamin, Chloe, and Jeremy

Photo Credits: cover, front endpapers, pp. 18–19, © Bette S. Garber/Highway Images; title page, © Mark E. Gibson/Visuals Unlimited; p. 6, David Paterson/Corbis; p. 8, Joseph Sohm, ChromoSohm, Inc./Corbis; p. 11, Neil Rabinowitz/Corbis; pp. 12–13, © John Sohlden/Visuals Unlimited; p. 14, Gehl Company/Corbis; pp. 17, 21, Roger Ressmeyer/© Corbis; pp. 22–23, Patrick Bennett/Corbis; pp. 24–25, CORBIS/Kevin R. Morris; p. 25, CORBIS/Philip James Corwin; pp 26–27, © Steve Strickland/Visuals Unlimited; pp. 28–29, © 1997 Jim Regan/Dembinsky Photo Assoc.; pp. 30, 31, © Beryl Goldberg, Photographer; pp. 32–33, Christine Osborne/Corbis; p. 35, © C. L. Smith/Visuals Unlimited; p. 36, Richard Hamilton Smith/Corbis; back endpapers: left, © Jeff Greenberg/Visuals Unlimited; right, © 1996 L. Linkhardt/Visuals Unlimited

Seymour Simon's Book of Trucks Copyright © 2000 by Seymour Simon Printed in Hong Kong. All rights reserved.

Library of Congress Cataloging-in-Publication Data
Simon, Seymour.
    Seymour Simon's book of trucks.
        p.   cm.
    Summary: Describes various kinds of trucks and their functions, including a log truck, cement mixer truck, and sanitation truck.
    ISBN 0-06-028473-0. — ISBN 0-06-028481-1 (lib. bdg.) — ISBN 0-06-446224-2 (pbk.)
    1. Trucks—Juvenile literature.   [1. Trucks.]   I. Title.   II. Title: Book of trucks.
TL230.15.S56   2000   99-14602
629.224—dc21   CIP

Typography by Al Cetta   ❖   Visit us on the World Wide Web! www.harperchildrens.com